Connecting Families
and the World through Photos

IMAGINE EVERYWHERE

J. Lawrence Graham

GREENLEAF
BOOK GROUP PRESS

A NOTE TO GROWN-UPS

In the pages that follow, you'll see some of my favorite photos that I've taken around the world. When I noticed connections between these images—whether in theme, color, action, or in other ways—I placed those pictures on the same page. The photos come from two dozen countries and states, and all seven continents.

The images in the book can be used to teach children in at least three ways:

LEARNING TO SPEAK: You can use the photos to teach younger children useful words and ideas. For example, while looking at the paired images of the momma and baby elephant and the mushrooms on the back cover, you can practice easy words such as "big" and "small," as well as more difficult words like "elephants" and "mushrooms."

LEARNING COMPARISONS: You might ask your five-year-old what is the same about any two pictures—that is, what words represent the images on any one page. For the lion and sea lion photos, you could point out things like "two," "whiskers," and "ears." Your child may even see additional similarities, concepts like "friends," "family," or "together."

You can also show why two things are not the same. For example, in the same lion and sea lion photos, you can point out the difference between "asleep" and "awake." Perhaps your child's understanding of the difference will help you get more sleep!

CREATIVE THINKING: An excellent tool for stimulating creative thinking is a deeper comparison of the images. Thinking and talking about all of the different kinds of connections and differences (beyond what we first see) changes the way our brains work. Making the brain work on new problems is a wonderful thing—a kind of mental exercise. And even the youngest kids know that exercise is good. For example, if you think a bit more about the elephants and mushrooms, you could talk about words like "animal" and "vegetable" or "savanna" versus "rain forest."

This book is a way to excite your children's interest in the bigger world—other places, other people and their families, other cultures, and other creatures from around the planet and beyond. Older readers may recognize places from their own world travels. Have fun guessing!

At the end of the book, there is a list of connecting terms and a little history about each of the pairs of photos, including their locations. But no doubt, you will come up with your own ideas about how to use these images to teach and interact with the special children in your life. So let your kids' (and your) imaginations go wild! How will you connect and compare these special photos from everywhere?

HOW MANY SHE LIONS

AND SEA LIONS DO YOU SEE?

How many kangaroos are looking at you?
Can you find a baby or two?
They're called joeys!
A group of kangaroos is called a mob.

Sea otters also live in
families, often called a raft.

WHERE DO YOU take NAPS? A MOMMA HIPPO LOOKS COMFY.

JUST LIKE HIPPOS, ZEBRAS ARE ANOTHER HORSE-LIKE AFRICAN ANIMAL THAT LIVE IN BIG FAMILIES. ARE THE ZEBRAS LOOKING AT YOU?

Do animals smile?
How about this giant tortoise?

I think a giant panda can! Do you?

CAN YOU RUN AS FAST AS A CHEETAH?

ARE YOU AS TALL AS A GIRAFFE?
CAN YOU SPOT HOW BOTH ANIMALS ARE THE SAME?

Do you like
taking a bath?
Bears do. Some even
eat in the tub.

GRIZZLY BEARS CAN BE BROWN, BUT SOME ARE WHITE.
THEY ARE DIFFERENT COLORS, JUST LIKE PEOPLE.

DO YOU RACE YOUR FRIENDS? DOLPHINS DO.

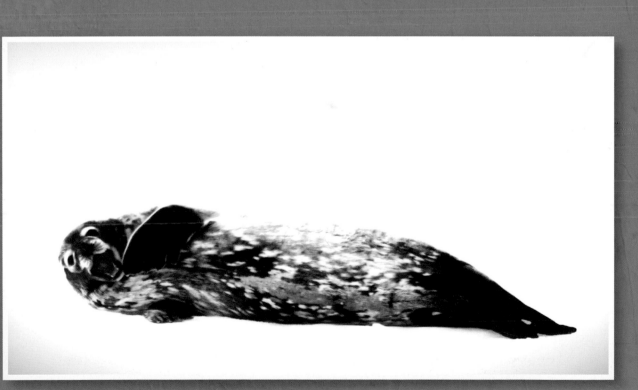

DOES THIS WEDDELL SEAL'S FACE LOOK LIKE A CAT'S?
IS IT SLEEPY?

DO YOU THINK PUFFINS eat MUFFINS?

DO YOU SLEEP IN a tree?

WHAT COLOR ARE
YOUR SHOES?
DO YOU HAVE ANY
BLUE ONES?

DOES THE
TRICOLORED HERON
HAVE FUR?

See the BEAUTY.

PEOPLE CAN
MAKE BEAUTIFUL
THINGS!

Sisters at play and at work.

Who would you like to play with today?

Boats are for work. Boats are for play.

How many are afloat in this boat?

PLAYING GAMES IS FUN AS YOU MAY.

DO YOU HAVE TIME TO PLAY TODAY?

Two grandfathers:

The boatman
watches for waves.

The artist makes
waves in the
princess's hair.

PEEKING THROUGH A
WINDOW . . . WHO'S
COMING HOME?

HOW MANY ARE
PEERING THROUGH THE
DOORWAY, ANYWAY?

THREE WOMEN
LAUGHING TOGETHER!

DO YOU THINK
TOWERING ROCKS
TALK TO EACH
OTHER?

DO YOU SEE THE TWINS?

HOW MANY ARE IN THIS FAMILY?

HOT, HOT SUN . . .

COLD, COLD SNOW. WHERE WOULD YOU LIKE TO GROW?

A little WATERFALL in a beautiful PLACE!

DOZENS OF tiNY PEOPLE see GIANT WATERFALLS that take UP the WHOLE PLACE!

HAVE YOU EVER SEEN THE STARS SURROUNDED BY GREEN?

HAVE YOU EVER SEEN A STAR COVERED BY A GREEN-CHEESE MOON?

FOR CURIOUS GROWN-UPS (AND KIDS)

Here are some suggested connecting words and fun facts about the photos.
How many connecting words can you add?

**CONNECTING WORDS—SIZES, GROWING, PARENT, CHILD,
SHELTER, SAFETY, PROTECTION**

A growing family of mushrooms in New Zealand are shown beside an elephant family in Tanzania. The orange caps on the mushrooms make them hard to miss (and squash!) along the hiking paths on the South Island near Queenstown. It would be very hard to miss even the tiniest baby elephant, and its mom would definitely not let you step on it!

**CONNECTING WORDS—LIONS, PAIR, BROWN, EARS, WHISKERS,
COMPANIONS, MAMMALS**

Lionesses in Tanzania thinking about food. Are the sea lions that live on the Galapagos Islands also dreaming about food? One of these friendly sea lions shuffled up onto the beach and actually laid its head on the legs of a napping woman! It would not be a good idea to get that close to an African lion!

CONNECTING WORDS—together, family, group, watching, closeness

A group of kangaroos is called a "mob." This photo shows a mob of eight Eastern Gray kangaroos in Queensland, Australia. Groups of otters are called "rafts." This raft of otters has gathered in Aialik Bay in Alaska. Both groups look like they enjoy playing.

CONNECTING WORDS—HORSE-LIKE, herds, Africa, four-legged, grazers, vegetarians

A group of hippos is called a "bloat." Sounds funny, doesn't it? Although they may not look it, hippos can be very dangerous, so you don't want to walk right up and pet one of these big creatures. Did you know that "hippo" means "horse" in Greek? Both the hippos and the zebras were photographed in Kenya, near or in the Mara River.

CONNECTING WORDS—HAPPY, round, rare, endangered, large, age, slow

The Galapagos tortoise in this photo is about 100 years old and weighs about 500 pounds. The giant panda weighs about half that and only lives about 20 years. This tortoise lives in Ecuador, and the panda lives on the other side of the world in China. They both love their vegetables—grasses and other greens for the tortoise and bamboo (also a kind of grass) for the panda.

CONNECTING WORDS—SPOTS, CAMOUFLAGE, AFRICA, SAVANNA,
EXCEPTIONAL, WORLD RECORD HOLDERS

The cheetahs are the fastest runners on the planet. In a sprint, they can reach 70 mph—that is freeway fast. After a sprint to catch hoofed prey, they take long, lazy naps, as shown in this photo snapped in Kenya. The giraffes are the tallest animals in the world. Here it looks like a mom is teaching her kids to dance. They like eating the tops of these Kenyan trees.

CONNECTING WORDS—GRIZZLY (OR BROWN) BEARS, KIN, SWIMMERS,
DIVERSITY IN COLOR AND AGE

These glorious bears live beside one another in and around Crescent Lake near Mount Redoubt in Alaska. The many salmon there are the main part of their diet much of the year. They hibernate about six months a year. Wet grizzly bears look skinny, but they can weigh up to 600 pounds and their claws can grow to four inches. Yikes!

CONNECTING WORDS—FISH, PREDATORS, MAMMALS, SWIM,
JUMP (IN AND INTO THE WATER)

Bottlenose dolphins live around the world, but these are from the Pacific Ocean just off Southern California. It seems the dolphins have the most fun of any animal species. In this photo they were racing the boat I was aboard and each other. Pods of dolphins hunt fish, jump, and play games. The only place you can't find a dolphin is near Antarctica. But you can find fat (1,000 pounds), lazy Weddell seals on the empty ice (my adventurous daughter Grace Graham took this photo).

CONNECTING WORDS—FEATHERS, BEAKS, VISION, STARING, FISH FOOD

The birds on the left are puffins living together on a rocky Icelandic island, where they are nesting in crevices and burrows. The baby birds on the right are reddish egrets from the Yucatan Peninsula in Mexico. Both types of birds need great vision to hunt for food and use their colorful feathers to fly.

CONNECTING WORDS—HUNTERS, FOWL, BLUE, WATER, FEET

Some of the most colorful birds of the Galapagos are the blue-footed boobies (yep, that's really their name!). The photo of the young, snake-skinny tricolored heron was taken on the Yucatan Peninsula in Mexico. Its feathers are bluish-gray, purple, and white. Both birds find food in the water. The boobies dive from the air at super speed. But the tricolored herons wade around in the shallows. Both birds mostly eat fish, but we have witnessed a heron swallowing a big rat. Yum!

CONNECTING WORDS—WOMEN, FACES, BEAUTY, DECORATION, ADORNMENT, EXOTIC

This young Maasai woman we met in Tanzania was all dressed up for a party. She was happy to pose for a picture with her favorite accessories on display. In the next photo, you see the sources of the colorful clothes the three Inca sisters wear. Both photos were taken in Peru on the road between Cuzco and Machu Picchu, high up in the Andes Mountains. The dyes make the yarns used to create the jackets' brilliant colors.

CONNECTING WORDS—SMILES, SISTERS, PINK, HAIR, MULTICOLORED, FASHION

The happy children from Peru smile like the Yao women near Guilin, China. The Yao women put up their extremely long, flowing black hair so it looks like a hat. The brilliant colors of their clothes look like those of their "little sisters" in Peru, even though they live a wide ocean apart.

CONNECTING WORDS—BOATS, FARMERS, RIVER, BAY, HANDCRAFTED, FLOATING

The men on the left are taking the produce from their family farm to the market across the Li River, near Guilin, China. Their handcrafted bamboo boat looks like it might sink, but they are safe because the river never gets very rough. In a back bay in Belize in Central America, a Mennonite farmer and his kids do a little fishing in the tiny boat they also made.

CONNECTING WORDS—FUN, PASTIME, GAME TIME, FRIENDS, NUMBERS, HANDS, POINTING

Chess and dominos are favorite board games in Havana, Cuba. They're fun and both help with math and strategic thinking skills. The huge clock is a vestige of the old train station that has been converted into the Musée d'Orsay in Paris. Kids from around the world have fun and build their imaginations when they pay a visit to that spectacular place.

CONNECTING WORDS—GRANDFATHERS, GRAY, COLORFUL, WORKING, FACES, PROUD

Near Montego Bay in Jamaica, you can take a boat ride with this local man. His long hair, called dreadlocks, is under his big hat in the photo. The street artist in Siena, Italy, has wild and crazy hair, but the sleeping beauty he paints with his chalks is splendid.

CONNECTING WORDS—GRANDDAUGHTERS, SUNLIGHT, DOORS, CURIOSITY, VIEW, OUTLOOK, OUTSIDE

A little girl in Coronado, California, is looking out the backdoor window, probably wondering, "What's going on out there?" Or perhaps she's waiting for a parent to come home. Next, with her friends in the background, older girls are looking at the light at the end of a tunnel in ruins near Angkor Wat in Cambodia.

CONNECTING WORDS—GOSSIP, STRAIT, TALKING, SCENERY, UNIFORM, CLUTCH

The photo of three women laughing and talking was taken on a boat crossing the Bosporus Strait on a windy day near Istanbul, Turkey. Perhaps they were gossiping? The 300-feet tall stand of rocks in Arches National Park near Moab, Utah, has been named the Three Gossips. Both places are wonderful sights to see.

CONNECTING WORDS—TOWER, SPECTACULAR, TALL, LORE, CONSTRUCTION

Devils Tower standing tall in northern Wyoming rivals the Three Gossips among Mother Nature's greatest natural constructions in the United States. Native Americans argue It's better called "Lodge of the Bears." This tower is millions of years old. In the second photo, three kids stand next to a parent in Giza, Egypt. The pyramids are only about four thousand years old.

CONNECTING WORDS—TREES, OXYGEN, LEAVES, WINTER, SUMMER, SEASONS, MOUNTAINS, FLORA

The bright green ground behind the African tree means there is a swamp in the otherwise very brown Tarangire National Park in Tanzania. Kitibong Hill is in the background. The stand of birches near Fairbanks, Alaska, reminds me of a general inspecting troops before battle. It also makes one wonder if trees have families.

CONNECTING WORDS—WATER, FALLING, RIVER,
NOURISHMENT, DANGEROUS, HIGH

Compared to Tanzania, the water is easier to see in the snowy Yosemite Valley, another national park, but located in the United States. Such flora give us many beautiful colors, smells, shapes, and even the air we breathe. Thanks, trees! And thank the Iguazu River that makes part of the border between Argentina and Brazil for providing so much water. It is the largest waterfall system in the world.

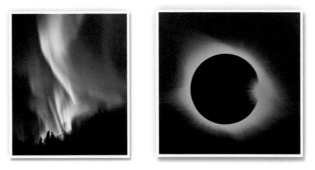

CONNECTING WORDS—SUNS, STARS, SOLAR SYSTEM,
ENERGY, HEAVENLY, TIMING, PREDICTION

If we're talking about imagining "everywhere," we have to include the cosmos. First are the "northern lights," the aurora borealis, shown here in Alaska. But also notice the stars and galaxies in the forever background. In the second photo, you can see the sun peeking from behind the eclipsing moon. That image comes from the total lunar eclipse of 2017 viewed from Great Falls, Idaho. It seems to show the grandfather sun, the Mother Earth we stand on, and the grand moon child we love. What fun!

ABOUT THE AUTHOR/PHOTOGRAPHER

J. Lawrence Graham is an educator, author, and photographer. He has traveled all over the world, teaching people how different cultures can get along and do business together. Lawrence has a wife, four children, two grandchildren, and two big, fluffy dogs. He has written nine books. This is his second book for children, and he really hopes you and the kids you know like it!

To see more of Lawrence's photographs, please visit his website at GrahamGalleries.com. Lawrence's other books for and about families are:

The Great Squirrel Burglar (for kids)
All in the Family: A Practical Guide to Successful Multigenerational Living
Charlotte's War (a historical novel)

ACKNOWLEDGMENTS

So much thanks to the following:

Kelly Herrity, a coauthor on an earlier version of this book for which she provided wonderful design work and prose.

Lynda Lawrence, a coauthor and colleague at the University of California, who introduced me to the concept of random juxtaposition as a means of stimulating creative thinking and invention.

My daughter Grace Graham, who spent two seasons at McMurdo Station in Antarctica, for contributing her photo of the Weddell seal.

Thanks also to Emily Graham, also my daughter, whose peek out the window in Coronado in 1974 got me started in this endeavor.

Also, the folks at Greenleaf Book Group have been wonderful teammates on this project: Erin Brown, Justin Branch, Neil Gonzalez, and Leah Pierre.

Published by Greenleaf Book Group Press
Austin, TX
www.gbgpress.com

Distributed by Greenleaf Book Group

For ordering information or special discounts for bulk purchases, please contact Greenleaf Book Group at PO Box 91869, Austin, TX 78709, 512.891.6100.

Design and composition by Greenleaf Book Group
Cover design by Greenleaf Book Group

Publisher's Cataloging-in-Publication data is available.

Print ISBN: 979-8-88645-119-1
eBook ISBN: 979-8-88645-122-1

To offset the number of trees consumed in the printing of our books, Greenleaf donates a portion of the proceeds from each printing to the Arbor Day Foundation. Greenleaf Book Group has replaced over 50,000 trees since 2007.

Manufactured through Asia Pacific Offset on acid-free paper
Manufactured in China, on May 2023
Batch No. APO-2023- Q23020448

23 24 25 26 27 28 29   10 9 8 7 6 5 4 3 2 1

First Edition